ANTHONY DAVIS

VIOLIN SONATA

for Violin and Piano

ED-3914

First Printing: March 1995

G. SCHIRMER, Inc.

DISTRIBUTED BY

HAL•LEONARD CORPORATION

7777 W. BLUEMOUND RD. P.O. BOX 13819 MILWAUKEE, WI 53213

duration: ca. 20 minutes

Commissioned by the Carnegie Hall Centennial Commission,
made possible, in part, by a challenge III grant from
the National Endowment for the Arts and with support from AT & T.

Premiere performance: February 3, 1991,
Michelle Makarski, violin, Brent McMunn, piano

VIOLIN SONATA
I

Anthony Davis

II

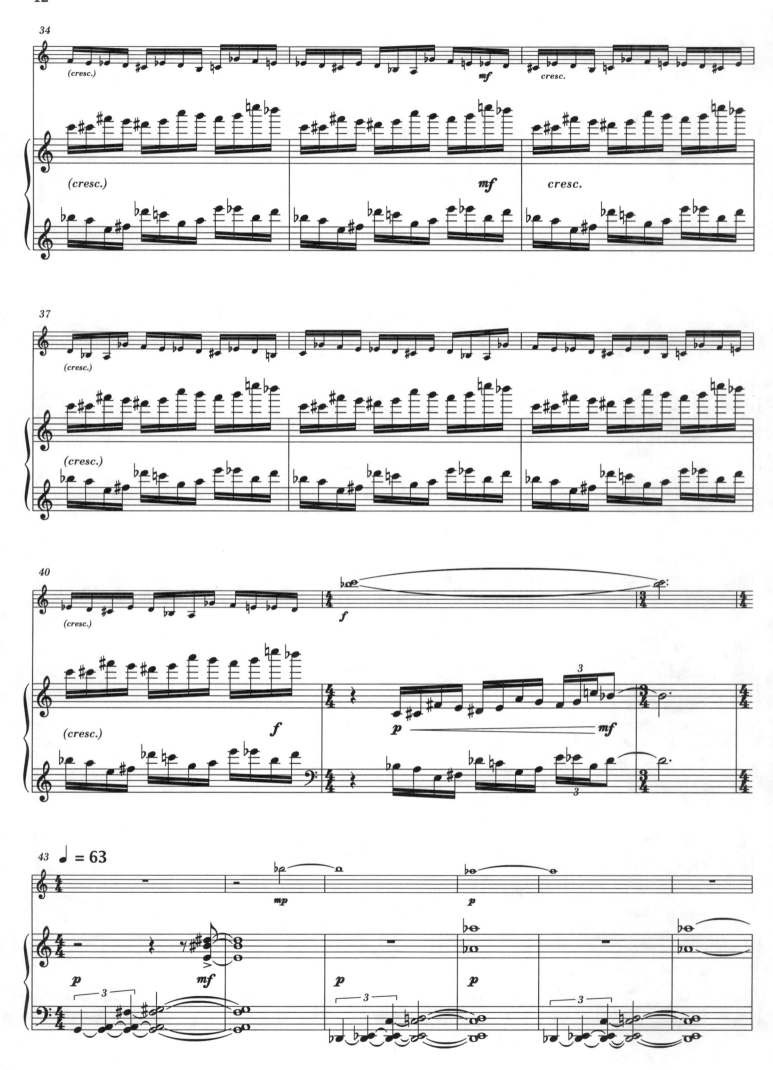

* Play ad lib. in a manner similar to the type of figuration in this movement.

* Optional: repeat these three measures *ad lib.* if the Violinist wishes to extend the improvisation.

III